WOMEN: THE HEARTBEAT OF SPORT

Also by Manisha Tailor
Dream Like Me: *South Asian Football Trailblazers* (2022)

WOMEN THE HEART BEAT OF SPORT

MANISHA TAILOR

HopeRoad Publishing
17 Kings Avenue
Leeds LS6 1QS
www.hoperoadpublishing.com
First published in Great Britain by HopeRoad 2025
Copyright © 2025 Manisha Tailor

The right of Manisha Tailor to be identified as the author of this work has been asserted by her in accordance with the Copyright, Designs and Patents Act 1988. All rights reserved. No part of this book may be reproduced, stored in a retrieval system or transmitted in any form or by any means, electronic, mechanical, photocopying, recording or otherwise, without the prior permission of the publishers.

This book is sold subject to the condition that it shall not, by way of trade or otherwise, be lent, re-sold, hired out or otherwise circulated without the publisher's prior consent in any form of binding or cover other than that in which it is published and without a similar condition including this condition being imposed on the subsequent purchaser.
A CIP catalogue record for this book is available from the British Library

ISBN: 978-1-913109-51-6
E-ISBN: 978-1-913109-49-3

To my mum, dad, brother and sister for their continued support;
I wouldn't be where I am without you.

To my friend and mentor Chris Ramsey, thank you for always motivating and
challenging me to think outside of the box.

To all the women in sport that have provided me with an opportunity to share
strong, bold and wonderful stories; let these inspire the future
generations of girls and women in sport.

'I raise up my voice – not so I can shout but so that those without a voice can be heard...we cannot succeed when half of us are held back'

MALALA YOUSAFZAI

DURVA VAHIA

Foreword

Life is more than what we do for a living, it's who we are that matters far more. The way we interact, care for, inspire and love each other is what the world will remember, long after we are gone. However, in Manisha's case, what she does for a living and who she is as a person combined, creates a powerhouse of a woman and role model. A trailblazer with a strong head and heart, gracefully taking up space in a world where women are conditioned to be small, is a legacy that will outlive her and many generations to come.

Manisha's impact ripples far beyond the people she interacts with, to people like me, who are an ocean away. Her non-traditional career choices, exceptional success and dedication to her cause, show us that with a clean heart and a clear head, if we set forth on our journey, we too can achieve success. The journey is different for all of us, and in this book, Manisha shares stories of other women who, like her, are strong, smart, resilient and inspiring. This book is a diamond mine of intelligence, elegance, strength and bravery, with stories of women breaking the glass ceiling and championing a pathway for generations of women to come.

While this book represents women from South Asia, its impact will be far wider. I hope people of all genders, ages, races, and ethnicities, have the opportunity to read this book. I hope that many young people can find role models and learn from the experiences of these women. I hope these young people can find themselves in these stories and embrace their power. But above all else, I hope to be these women. Thank you, Manisha, for all that you, and your work, bring to the world.

Durva Vahia

AISHA NAZIA

AISHA NAZIA

'Every barrier you face is an opportunity to rewrite the rules'

Aisha Nazia's journey began in the vibrant coastal town of Kozhikode, India, where football was more than just a sport – it was the heartbeat of the community. Today, she is a trail-blazer in global sports marketing and event management, with a career spanning multiple continents, working on premier events such as the F1 Saudi Arabian Grand Prix, Dakar Rally, GT World Challenge, Street Child World Cups, NBA Games, FIFA U17 World Cup, Indian Super League and so on. Aisha has established herself as a true titan in the world of sports, though this journey was by no means easy.

'My mother, a single parent, taught me resilience and independence – values that I carry with me every day. As a young girl in a society that believed sports were not for girls, I often felt like an outsider looking in.

'Then one day, everything changed. I watched my first Formula 1 race on TV. It was 2007, and Lewis Hamilton won his very first race in Canada. I remember staring at the screen, amazed by the speed, the skill, and most of all, the determination. If someone like Lewis could rise against the odds, maybe I could too. That's when I decided – I would build a life in sports, no matter how many barriers I had to break.'

Aisha, a qualified mechanical engineer, actively sought opportunities to transition into the sports sector and began her career in sports with Kerala Blasters and the Indian Super League, gaining invaluable experience in sports management, and setting the stage for her future successes in the global sports industry. Later pursuing the FIFA Master's Programme, an elite course in sports management, law and humanities, prepared her for a future managing some of the world's most prestigious sporting events.

She gained hands-on experience through impact initiatives like Football for Future and Street Child United, which deepened her understanding of sports' ability to transform communities. Her career on the global stage with FIFA, NBA, F1, GT and other major sporting events saw her transition from managing event operations to leading international marketing campaigns and driving the future of sports. Her role involves crafting integrated marketing strategies, managing fan engagement, and leading multi-million-dollar sponsorship campaigns.

'What I enjoy most is storytelling, connecting with fans worldwide and using sports as a platform to inspire change. Collaborating with diverse teams and executing campaigns that create lasting memories for audiences is deeply fulfilling as every event is a celebration of dreams, determination, and teamwork.'

Breaking into a male-dominated sports industry as an Indian woman is no small feat. She faced scepticism about her capabilities and cultural biases and found balancing the high demands of global event management, including extensive travel and tight deadlines, a test of adaptability and determination. However, each hurdle reinforced her commitment to creating equitable opportunities in sports for under-represented groups.

'There were times when people doubted me, simply because I was a woman or because I didn't fit into the traditional mould of a sports professional. I had to work twice as hard to prove myself. I learned that believing in yourself is the most powerful tool you can have.'

Sports, Aisha says, are like life. It's about overcoming setbacks and striving forward to achieve your dream. She believes that you should build a network of mentors and supporters who believe in your vision and remember that continuous learning is key – embrace new skills and perspectives as every setback can teach you something important.

LESSONS FOR GOOD MENTAL HEALTH: You are stronger than you think, and there's always light at the end of the tunnel. So, dream big. Don't let anyone tell you what you can or cannot do. Keep learning. Every challenge teaches you something new, embrace it. Find support. Surround yourself with people who believe in you and your vision. Take care of yourself. Life can be overwhelming, so take breaks and do things that make you happy.

PERSONAL MESSAGE: 'Your dreams are yours to follow, no matter what anyone says. Life won't always be easy, and challenges will come your way, but every obstacle is a chance to grow stronger. Never let fear or doubt stop you. Never stop chasing what excites you. You have the power to make a difference, inspire others, and leave your mark on the world. So be bold, stay curious, and go after what sets your heart on fire!'

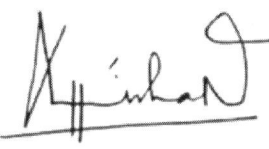

Questions to think about:

1. Why did Aisha feel like an 'outsider' within sport and how do you think this made her feel?

2. What inspired Aisha to take up a career in motorsport?

3. Can you name five influential female motorsport drivers and describe their achievements within the sport?

4. List and explain three key things that you have learned about brand management and marketing.

ALANA KING

ALANA KING

*'Spin it as hard as you can, give it a rip,
and do it with a smile on your face.'*

Alana King's family left one cricketing nation for another when her parents migrated from Chennai, India, to Australia in the 1980s. Alana was born in 1995 in Melbourne. Growing up, she tried several sports but after initially focusing on tennis, she followed her dad and older brother by taking up cricket.

'As every other kid, I started in the back garden, which moved quickly to the front garden as my brother and I maybe broke too many pot plants and a couple of windows as well,' says Alana.

Alana soon joined a club team, and her all-round talent stood out.

'My brother's coach said to my dad, "Your daughter can play. You need to bring her down to the club" says Alana. 'Mum and Dad were reluctant because there weren't any girls playing. I would be playing with all boys. They were a lot bigger and stronger than me at the same age, but I was a pretty persistent kid. They embraced me because I was just there to play cricket. . . I knew that they hated getting out to me in the nets, my teammates, so I knew how much the opposition hated it. I would hear comments like, "You got out to a girl" or, "She hit you for four."'

The cricket-mad youngster also played at school, but it wasn't until she was invited to a trial for the state of Victoria representative side that she realised there were all-girls teams.

'I thought, "Woah, this is cool," says Alana. 'There are 30 other girls playing the sport you love. That was a pretty eye-opening moment because I was like, "Where are all these girls playing?" There's none in my area.'

Alana eventually made the Victoria team and even received some treasured advice from the great Aussie leg spin bowler Shane Warne, who told her to

'Spin it as hard as you can, give it a rip, and do it with a smile on your face.'

After receiving her first contract at sixteen, Alana played for her home state for five years and considers loyalty one of her best traits. However, she ultimately felt she needed a change to boost her career, so she made the tough decision to move across the country to join the Perth Scorchers in Western Australia.

'Obviously, moving away from everyone was a big thing,' she says. 'My whole family is in Melbourne. The way our family and culture is, I miss people just popping over. I used to love popping over to my aunty's house on a random night and you just eat whatever is in the fridge and you make do. Those are the connections I miss.[But] I just had to try. . . I didn't want to have that regret later in my career.'

Happily, the sacrifice was worth it. In a stellar career, Alana has represented Australia in test, one-day, and Twenty20 cricket and has become a role model to her community and beyond.

'Whether you like it or not, the moment you step out onto the field in an elite environment you are going to be a role model because there are eyes on you,' she says. 'I have learned to accept what comes with that. I have just embraced it. . . If I can get one boy or girl to pick up the art of leg-spin because they see me on TV with some shades on, loving every minute when I take a wicket, that puts a big smile on my face.'

LESSONS FOR GOOD MENTAL HEALTH: 'Sometimes, you have to make sacrifices in order to succeed. Keep focus and be willing to give it your all.'

Questions to think about:

1. What does migration mean? Alana's parents migrated in the 1980s. Where did they migrate from and where did they migrate to?

2. Alana's parents were initially reluctant to let her play for a club. What was the reason for this?

3. There are now more opportunities for girls to play cricket and inspire them to play professionally if that is something that they wish to do. Can you name a female professional cricketer and describe what makes them inspiring?

4. Alana considers 'loyalty' one of her best traits. What is your best trait and why?

AMI PAREKH

AMI PAREKH

'Follow your heart and especially that sometimes quiet voice inside your head that tells you that you can actually do it.'

Ami Parekh was a rarity in her sport. Born into a Gujarati family in New Jersey, USA, her early passion for figure skating was a surprise. There were no athletes in her family, and in the patriarchal South Asian community, gender roles and career aspirations were clearly defined.

'Our parents are from a country where sport was not highly emphasized at the time they grew up,' says Ami. 'There are not many South Asians in figure skating, and it's a very Western sport. If your community doesn't understand what goes into a sport, they're less likely to support you.'

Of course, as a youngster, Ami wasn't aware of the cultural norms. She just loved to skate. Though she didn't make a promising start.

'I split my chin open, and I got stitches,' says Ami. 'So, I was pretty much done after that. But then, for some reason, I went back. And so, at nine, I started taking lessons. It started out as a recreational thing, but every time I learned something new, I got the thirst to learn more.'

With Ami's talent and her mother's support, she began to compete.

'It's very important to have family support,' she says. 'It was very helpful that my mum was always there with me. At every practice session, she videotaped me. I would study my videos. She would drive me to different places to get the full spectrum that's needed to excel at the sport.'

And excel she did. In India, she became an eight-time ladies' champion. And when India joined the International Skating Union (ISU), she was the first skater to represent India at the ISU Senior World Figure Skating Championships.

'Wearing a sari at the opening banquet and introducing our culture to the Western countries was cool and fun,' she says.

Getting to the top took dedication and sacrifice.

'You have to skate all year round; otherwise, you'll quickly lose your skills on the ice,' says Ami.

A hectic schedule wasn't Ami's only challenge. While her uniqueness got her noticed, it could also be a burden.

'I was one of the few, or sometimes the only one, in my environment that was an Indian elite figure skater,' she says. 'One of the challenges was highlighting what we bring to the table as Indians and South Asians on the ice. Being able to navigate that without being self-conscious was challenging because, of course, as a teenager, you want to fit in. And in my world, I didn't fit in anywhere at that time. I was different in the South Asian community, and I was different in the figure-skating community.'

But eventually, Ami embraced her differences and thrived as a figure-skating champion and coach, and later in the medical field, where her career has blossomed.

'I love pushing myself mentally and physically every day,' she says. 'Since being the best athlete possible can be extremely psychological, I worked on myself to divert my focus to the positive, focused on what my goals were, and planned exactly how I would reach them.'

Even as a doctor, she faced challenges in sports – mostly because she was the uncommon mother trainee who wanted to pursue sports medicine. 'After getting through many years of training as a mother, I was told that despite my qualifications and experiences, being a mother, especially of multiple children, was a considerably negative factor for one-year post-graduate sports medicine fellowship programmes.' Despite this, and now with three children, she has managed to help many people of all ages while practising sports medicine, on and off the playing field.

LESSONS FOR GOOD MENTAL HEALTH: 'Surround yourself with supportive people who understand and value your goals.'

PERSONAL MESSAGE: 'There may always be challenges along your journey, no matter what age you are, or what you have already achieved. Sticking to your goals and values, channelling your positivity by focusing on solutions, taking those baby steps, and knowing your allies will take you a long way! Mental flexibility and finding ways to enjoy the process can also bring amazing surprises in life.'

Questions to think about:

1. What is a figure skater?

2. Ami speaks about dedication and sacrifice. How did this enable her to excel in her sport?

3. What are some of the challenges that Ami faced during her journey in the sports world, and how did she overcome them?

4. Can you list three goals that you are focused on and the steps that you are going to take to achieve them?

ESHA NAYAR

ESHA NAYAR

'Be prepared to step outside your comfort zone. If you wish to succeed and improve, you need to be prepared to do so.'

Many successful people can point to a role model who lit their path to success. But when British Asian basketball player Esha Nayar looked around for inspiration as a youngster, she saw no one.

'I don't think I've ever really had anyone to look up to when I first started playing my sport,' says Esha. 'Not only did it lack females, it also lacked, and still does, players and coaches of a similar background to myself.'

With no one to guide her, Esha had to forge her own path. And it wasn't long before her potential was recognized, and she joined the England under-15s basketball talent programme.

'The training camps proved to be both a physical and mental challenge,' says Esha. 'Being surrounded by such high-calibre players was a great experience which pushed me to improve my skills.'

Of course, even at a junior level, sport can be ruthless, and Esha has faced her share of hurdles.

'I was once cut from the U16s first team to the second team,' she explains. 'There was controversy surrounding this decision as I was in the England talent programme at the time. Upon review, the club recognized their error. It was mentally challenging, but I continued to train and persevered through the situation.'

Embracing the ups and downs of the sport, Esha was able to rise through the ranks, assuming ever more responsibility as she did so.

'I am a player for the Manchester Mystics Division 1 women's team,' says Esha. 'I progressed through the ranks of playing in the U18's and had earned the role of team captain. I thoroughly enjoyed this opportunity as it has allowed me to take on a role of leadership and has assisted in me serving on the Basketball England's Future Youth Committee.'

As she's continued to play, Esha has become increasingly aware of her role as a trail-blazer and more outspoken about being one of the few South Asian women ever to play National League basketball. Now also a coach, frustratingly, she says she still gets compared to the star of the movie *Bend it like Beckham* even though she's a Hindu and not a Sikh, plays basketball instead of football, and is a real, not fictional, athlete.

However, Esha feels changing perceptions is all about perseverance. She also believes in having a confidante ready to listen when the going gets tough.

'Sometimes participating in a sport may be mentally challenging,' she says. 'If your sport starts to negatively affect your mental health, seriously consider talking to someone you feel comfortable talking to, such as a teammate or a coach. You can then identify what it is that may be affecting you negatively.'

Esha's is a story of self-belief and determination to realize her goals, even though she had no footsteps to follow. Breaking new ground, she also had to be flexible and adaptable. And that's the advice she offers to others.

'Be ready to persevere as your journey may be thrown off course due to factors that are completely out of your control,' she says. 'Also, be prepared to be working with a range of different people who come from a large range of different backgrounds.'

LESSONS FOR GOOD MENTAL HEALTH: Be prepared to step outside your comfort zone. If you wish to succeed and improve, you need to be prepared to do so.

PERSONAL MESSAGE: 'As I've grown older and had increased involvement with sport off the court, I am now prouder of what I have achieved off the court more than those from being on it. I feel as if the impact that you can have on people when doing things whilst not playing can help to inspire the younger generation of players. I want to ensure that everyone feels represented and comfortable within their sporting environment.'

Questions to think about:

1. Esha had to forge her own path in her sport. What key character traits would you say Esha embodies that allow her to maintain resilience?

2. When times got tough, what did Esha do to keep going? What do you do to maintain discipline?

3. Esha speaks of being a leader. What do you think makes a good leader and why? Name a leader that inspires you and provide a reason for your choice.

4. Esha is a role model, trying to change perceptions in her sport. As a change maker, what do you stand for? What is important to you? If you were asked to write a letter to a governing body based on what you have learned following reading Esha's story, what would you write?

GURPREET SOHI

GURPREET SOHI

'Pressure is a privilege'

A shining example of handling pressure is Gurpreet Sohi, a water polo player who represented Canada at the 2020 Summer Olympics in Tokyo, Japan.

Born in Delta, British Columbia, Gurpreet followed her older brother, Navjot, into the pool at the age of nine. It was a bold move, as when she began her water polo career, she could barely swim!

'When I started playing water polo, I was the tiniest player in the pool.' Gurpreet says. 'They had a rule that you could come to practice if you could swim a full lap of the pool. I couldn't even swim a full lap of the pool, but I still wanted to jump in and try!'

However, once she learned the basics, it became obvious that Gurpreet had talent. But that didn't mean she was automatically accepted by others, who, culturally speaking, saw her as a fish out of water.

'It used to be mixed age and gender because we didn't have enough players. I was a ten-year-old playing against sixteen-year-old Eastern European men,' Gurpreet says. 'And they would look at me, and they would laugh, and everyone would want to guard me because I was the easy one to guard. But this just motivated me to work even harder. I started to utilize other skills like speed, drive and critical thinking.'

Gurpreet thrived under the pressure of being underestimated. By the age of fourteen, she'd joined the ranks of the Canadian Water Polo youth team. She captained the girls' team for three years, helping them to a silver medal in the national high school competition and becoming a two-time All-Star. She also helped Canada claim a gold medal at the 2011 Youth Pan Am Games.

Looking back, Gurpreet realizes that her youthful success was an incredible achievement for someone from her cultural background. But at the time, she wasn't aware of being a groundbreaker. 'My mom has always been my role model. She was a beaming example of hard work and resilience. It was her support that allowed me to break barriers,' says Gurpreet.

While starring in the pool, Gurpreet also handled the pressure in the classroom. After high school, she earned a scholarship to study Human Biology at the prestigious Stanford University, where she won awards for academic excellence in all four years. She focused her degree on Global Health and Human Rights and even studied in Cambodia for a period of time. Meanwhile, she helped the Cardinals win back-to-back NCAA water polo championships, captaining the team in her senior year and earning an All-America Honorable Mention.

Since college, Gurpreet's passion for water polo has continued. She's competed in four FINA World League Super Finals, winning a silver medal in 2017, and was part of Canada's fourth-place finish at the FINA World League Super Final in 2021.

By all measures, her water polo career has been a triumph, and she's eternally grateful to her parents for their support and for giving her the freedom to walk her own path. 'I have my parents to thank for my success,' Gurpreet says. 'They're really open to whatever I want to do. . . and they're big advocates for other families to really allow their kids to explore athletics and see where that can take them.'

As she hangs up her swimsuit, her next journey lies in medical school. On her way to becoming a doctor, she reflects back on her water polo career, knowing that it instilled important lessons of grit, leadership and collaboration.

LESSONS FOR GOOD MENTAL HEALTH: 'Finding ways to manage under pressure have helped me to thrive. Developing adaptability can help you to manage in difficult situations.'

GURPREET SOHI

PERSONAL MESSAGE: 'Embrace pressure; it holds us accountable to our highest potential. Be bold, be resilient and chase your dreams. When things feel hard, lean on your friends and family. And most of all, hug your parents tight – they are often the unsung heroes of our successes.'

Questions to think about:

1. Name and describe three things that help you to manage pressure.

2. Why did Gurpreet's competitors laugh at her and what did she do to overcome this?

3. How many years did Gurpreet spend as captain for her school team? What do you think defines a good captain and why?

4. Gurpreet speaks of the support received from her parents. How has this support enabled her to achieve her dreams? What advice do her parents give to others?

HARLEEN KAUR

HARLEEN KAUR

'There's no quick fix or easy way to get good results, you have to put in the work, and hard work always pays off!'

Harleen Kaur is a British Asian fighter who's beaten opponents and ethnic stereotypes in equal measure.

Harleen took up karate when she was in Year five at primary school. It was her friend's birthday gift, and she had asked her to come along to the session. This became a regular thing, and they would attend every week until Harleen achieved her 2nd degree black belt in karate. Harleen then started competing in regional competitions, winning titles, and then going on to win national championships. In 2015, she was selected to represent England in the kickboxing world championships after winning gold at the British championships. She won silver at the world championships in 2015 and 2016.

As a South Asian female, kickboxing was an extremely untraditional path. What's more, she was fighting on two fronts, as an athlete and business owner. After graduating from Leeds Beckett University with a Sport and Exercise Sciences degree, she set up Club Ekta. The initial goal of the club was to empower women through sport and physical activity, but it's now expanded its services to children and young people.

'Club Ekta is a women's club that supports and empowers women in Bradford and Leeds,' Harleen explains. 'The word Ekta is derived from the Sanskrit transcript, which means "unity". Growing up, I found it hard to find relatable role models. It's good for young girls to look up to people from similar backgrounds, and a club like this brings together a network of inspirational females where not only does it benefit young girls, but it also benefits women who want to achieve and get back to society but are not sure where to start their careers.' In the business world, Harleen has battled some of the same preconceptions that she did when starting her fighting career. But she's been determined to follow her passions, despite the numerous challenges.

'I felt like it's hard to have my voice heard and not being taken seriously as a young female in business. I think women are still under-represented in many fields. In the beginning, the lack of business support was hard. A year later, I found out I had set up the wrong type of CIC and had to set up a new one, obviously losing a year's worth of trading history, which had a significant impact on work.

'However, I feel like being an entrepreneur is about learning on the job, and there's nothing you cannot bounce back from.'

Aside from her sporting and professional endeavours, Harleen is also a keen volunteer for a sports charity. Each summer, she visits Punjab in North India, where she teaches life skills, English, and self-defence.

In all aspects, her journey so far has been characterized by high achievement. In mind and body, she's excelled. Her recipe for success is focus, application, and a strong mindset. And to those hoping to follow her example in their own fields, she's proof positive that that combination packs a powerful punch.

'I think we should all have the mindset that "better" never stops. As a person, we should always be learning new things or looking for ways to improve existing skillsets. There's no quick fix or easy way to get good results, you have to put in the work, and hard work always pays off!'

LESSONS FOR GOOD MENTAL HEALTH: Believe in yourself and have a positive mental attitude towards everything. It's so important to focus on the present moment.

PERSONAL MESSAGE: 'Success isn't just about what you accomplish in life, it's about what you inspire others to do, so don't just break barriers, build bridges for others to cross.'

Questions to think about:

1. Harleen started her learning in karate, before representing England in kickboxing. Can you do some research and list some similarities and differences within each sport?

2. Harleen proves that skills can be transferable. Can you list some important interpersonal and life skills that can help you in different situations?

3. What do you do to help you maintain a strong mindset?

4. How do you focus on the 'present' moment and what are the benefits of doing this?

HARMINDER KAUR BEHAL

HARMINDER KAUR BEHAL

'Your journey is unique to you.
Believe in yourself and enjoy the journey.'

Football scout Harminder Kaur Behal is one of the unsung heroes of the game. Her background is Sikh, Punjabi and British South Asian, and her love for the sport has family roots.

'It was a family tradition to watch all FA Cup games and international games on TV when I was growing up, and I also played football from a young age.

'I gained my FA Level 1 in Coaching and FA Level 2 in National Talent Identification and Scouting. I really enjoyed the talent ID content as I have experience of working in human resources and teaching areas which are all people development focused, and felt I could use my transferable skills and experience alongside learning more about talent identification, mentoring, and development,' says Harminder.

Along with her courses, Harminder worked at club level within a boys' academy. Later, at an agency, she got hands-on experience in live and video scouting. She was also responsible for the women's player recruitment strategy.

For a scout there is a lot of work that goes on behind the scenes which can involve long hours, player development discussions, planning and preparing games/players to observe and monitor, and leagues to cover, along with journeys to different parts of the country within a short space of time.

'My current role as a talent reporter entails watching live and video games working across a variety of age groups with a main focus on the youth-development-phase and professional-development-phase age groups for England Women. I enjoy going out to live games and then being able to share my observations and reports about the players in the England Women's pathway. It is great to be a part of a supportive team with opportunities for personal development and growth,' she says.

Football has also enabled her to travel, meet and learn so much from different communities, clubs and individuals around the world and they have been incredible personal and professional life-changing experiences. Being a part of a global network of growing the women's game is one of the greatest rewards of working in the game.

As a South Asian woman, Harminder is breaking new ground in scouting with her gender and ethnicity, and her game plan for success was learned in the trenches.

The best parts of the journey have been learning and development, embracing the unknown, believing in herself and also learning from those around her.

Harminder says asking questions and networking are key to building connections and learning about the industry. Dedication and perseverance, she says, are essential. Patience, perspective, continual learning, a strong support system and enjoying the journey are some of her key components to developing within talent ID.

For Harminder, making the talent pathway more diverse is the change she wants to help create in the game to ensure talent from all different backgrounds are given the access, support and opportunity to succeed.

LESSONS FOR GOOD MENTAL HEALTH: It's important to never compare your journey to anyone else. Your journey is unique to you. Always believe in yourself, build a support network, feel good in what you are doing and enjoy the journey.

PERSONAL MESSAGE: 'Enjoy the journey, embrace every experience and stay curious as if it is teaching you something, that includes the good, the lessons, and the in-between. Try not to overthink or worry too much if things don't always go to plan or mistakes are made along the way, reflect, adapt and learn from them as I feel these skills have allowed me to keep refining the lifelong learner's mindset. I've learnt a lot from setbacks, failures and always used them to fuel my next move. It's important to celebrate your success and take learnings from these times too. If you can – look to share with others to continue paving the way forward and contribute to something greater than yourself."

Harminder Kaur Behal

Questions to think about:

1. What do you think makes a good talent ID scout and why?

2. Harminder didn't have any visible role models in talent ID and has now become one for others. Who do you consider to be your role model and why?

3. Harminder speaks about having a sense of direction. If you had a choice, what would be your most desired job and what are the steps that you would take to achieve this? Map out your action plan.

4. Consistency is key. List five daily habits that can help you to maintain consistency.

ISA GUHA

ISA GUHA

'I want to be the best I can be, so I am always looking for ways to improve my performance.'

Isa Guha's cricket career began at eight-years-old in High Wycombe, England, where her parents had settled after arriving from Calcutta, India, in the 1970s. There were no girls' teams to play for, so she initially played with boys.

'The fact that my parents never saw it as an issue when some traditional families might have done kind of helped the situation as no one else then saw it as an issue.'

But being the only girl of Asian descent did have its drawbacks, and Isa sometimes had to dig deep to stick at it.

'It probably helped my cricket because I was spending so much time out of my comfort zone, but it still came with the same desires of wanting to fit in,' she says. 'There were times when I was twelve or thirteen when I wanted to quit the game because I felt like I wasn't.'

But Isa persisted as part of the Development England side as a twelve-year-old, from where her progress was rapid. At sixteen, she became the first woman of Indian heritage to play for England, making her one-day international debut in the Women's European Championship. A year later, she made her Test debut. She was also named BBC Asian Sports Personality of the Year.

She'd be a fixture of the England team for a decade, earning a combined 231 caps, which included winning the World Cup and World T20. Isa's playing career was a huge success, but she admits to turning a blind eye to some of the negatives.

'I think you look back on times where people have perhaps been discriminatory towards you on the journey and many times I perhaps blocked it out,' she says. 'I tried to ignore it but it did create a self-conscious feeling for me at times which I probably wasn't as alert to in the moment. Essentially you want to fit in, and you want to fit into society so you brush it to one side. Would I have been able to pursue playing at the highest level if I [had] allowed it to get to me? Probably not, but I can see the impact it had on me now in terms of the pressure I placed on myself.'

Isa retired from international cricket in 2012. Soon after, she joined the media, going on to become an award-winning cricket commentator and broadcaster. Though the transition wasn't easy.

'When I started doing commentary, I wasn't very good, but with time and experience I learned the different aspects of high-quality broadcasting.'

As the lead presenter for BBC Cricket and the daytime Wimbledon slot, Isa's job requires self-confidence and unflappable poise, whatever happens behind the camera.

'It's chaos behind the scenes, but it's very fulfilling working with directors and producers to get the best out of guests, and to deliver something for your audience that's informative and entertaining,' she says. 'When things go wrong, I have to navigate the way through, making it appear seamless: that is so satisfying.'

In addition to broadcasting, Isa is committed to inspiring and empowering the next generation of female cricketers through her charity, Take Her Lead, which was founded in memory of her mum, Roma. The charity seeks to enable a more inclusive culture for women and girls, by empowering, amplifying and connecting across the cricket community.

'We all have women in our lives that we draw inspiration from and mine was my mum, Roma. She gave me the advice I needed to continue playing at twelve and so we want to provide that support to other young girls starting out in the game and also to build a connection for those from disadvantaged communities to say "cricket is a game for me". It's exciting to see the impact we've had already in a short amount of time. Ultimately to be part of the change to help women and girls feel like they belong is something that I know my mum would be proud of.'

ISA GUHA

LESSONS FOR GOOD MENTAL HEALTH: Find time for whatever it is that makes you feel good and alive. Whether it's a walk in nature, live music, dinner with friends, always try and find time to do it.

PERSONAL MESSAGE: 'In a world where there are increasing opportunities and it's difficult to know which direction to take, I think it's important to nail down your values. You're not always going to land on what you want but it's as much about figuring out what you don't want to do that leans you towards the right path. I've always seen failure as a learning experience so all you have to do is have the courage to try.'

Questions to think about:

1. Isa spent much of her early cricket career playing with boys. How has sport changed to provide equal access for both boys and girls?

2. Isa made history by becoming the first woman of Indian heritage to play for England. How do you think she must have been feeling and why is this moment in history so special?

3. What life skills can cricket teach you? Can you describe them and how you would use them in your everyday life?

4. Can you name some of Isa's key attributes?

JIYA RAI

JIYA RAI

'We had two options: hide our child at home or have her step outside.'

Jiya Rai was dealt a pretty tough hand. At the age of two, she was diagnosed with autism spectrum disorder (ASD) and a problem with speech development that unfortunately drew ridicule from some children and adults.

'When Jiya still hadn't started talking at age two, and kept to herself when other kids were around, [we] met a doctor who diagnosed autism,' says her father, Madan Rai, an Indian Navy officer working in Mumbai.

On doctors' advice, her parents started Jiya on a swim training programme.

'We had two options,' says her father. 'Hide our child at home or have her step outside. It was harsh to put her into water at the age of two, but I had to do that for her.'

Though swimming requires training and can be a tough discipline to teach a child with autism, Jiya proved to be a natural swimmer and immediately fell in love with the water. It wasn't long before she was entered in swimming events, though she didn't fully understand the idea of competition.

'Initially, she couldn't tell if she had won or lost,' says her mother, Rachana. 'Gradually, she began to understand that trophies meant wins. Then she began flashing a victory sign after crossing the line first.'

Jiya's success in the pool eventually caught the eye of a Mumbai swimming coach who thought her incredible stamina would make her a perfect fit for long-distance swimming. And with that, her career in open-water swimming began.

In no time, Jiya started claiming victory after victory and record after record, despite being nonverbal and unfamiliar with the concept of distance.

'We design posters with the start and finish point for her swims, be it a lighthouse or a bridge,' says her father. 'We put it up on the boats that follow her, so it's always in her head. Once she spots it in the distance while swimming, she will turn to us and smile. And then nothing will stop her.'

Jiya's achievements garnered national attention. Most notably, when she became the youngest and fastest female swimmer in history to cross the Palk Strait, the 29-kilometre sea channel connecting India and Sri Lanka, which she swam in thirteen hours and ten minutes. She also made the Guinness Book of World Records as the youngest and only female member of the team that completed the world's longest open-water sea-swimming relay by covering a distance of 1100 kilometres.

By overcoming the common limitations of autism in such a spectacular manner, Jiya has become an inspiration to many. In 2022, she received the prestigious Pradhan Mantri Rashtriya Bal Puraskar, India's highest award for an under-eighteen-year-old. Then, in 2023, she was honoured with a Shriver-Kennedy Student Achievement Award, presented by the Division on Autism and Developmental Disabilities, the world's largest international professional organization dedicated to supporting the needs of students with disabilities.

Today, Jiya is no longer the figure of fun she was cruelly made to be as a toddler. Instead, she's a successful and accomplished teenager with a legion of admirers.

LESSONS FOR GOOD MENTAL HEALTH: A teacher once told Jiya it's OK if she doesn't understand history; she'll soon be writing her own history and so can you.

Questions to think about:

1. Jiya found swimming to be a safe space for her and found herself to be a natural swimmer. What does a safe space mean to you? How is a safe space helpful to your mental health?

2. How did Jiya's journey in open water begin?

3. What does it mean to be nonverbal? How has Jiya overcome this?

4. What strategies have Jiya's parents put in place to help her understand the concept of distance?

KARENJEET KAUR BAINS

KARENJEET KAUR BAINS

'Be proud of where you come from.
It's only going to propel you forward.'

Karenjeet Kaur Bains is the embodiment of a strong Asian woman. Born in Warwick, England, to parents from the Punjab region of India, she didn't face the resistance to her sporting ambitions that other girls in the Asian community often do. 'My parents never stopped me. They always pushed me equally,' says Karenjeet.

That parental support was born from experience. In his youth, her father was a powerlifter and bodybuilder. Her mother won local honours in the hammer, discus, and shot put, and her older twin brothers competed at national level in the 400-metre hurdles. Karanjeet herself was a teenage sprint champion, but it was powerlifting that ultimately grabbed her interest. So, at the age of seventeen, she began training at her dad's homemade gym with him as her coach.

'We have a really fantastic relationship,' says Karenjeet. 'Obviously, my dad always says he considers himself a dad first and then a coach second. It's really nice how it's almost developed quite from the grassroots – when I was a schoolgirl with a dream.'

Of course, powerlifting is a male-dominated sport, and even as her career literally went from strength to strength, she had to deal with the same old preconceptions, even at her dad's gym.

'Quite an elderly man came across to my dad. This guy didn't know I was British champion at the time. And he said to my dad, "I'm not sure there's going to be dumbbells small enough for your daughter." And my dad said, "I'm not sure there's going to be dumbbells big enough for my daughter." And I think from that moment and that comment, it was like, I really need to turn the tide.'

And she turned the tide in a big way. Naturally strong, with a dedication to training and good technique, she won title after title, breaking barriers, smashing stereotypes, and eventually making history.

'Becoming the first Sikh female to represent Great Britain at the World and European championships, that was the stepping stone to shatter any glass ceilings about what a female can achieve,' she says. 'Never judge a book by its cover. Never have any preconceptions about what a female's strength can be.'

Her success has not come at the expense of her religion and heritage but partly because of it. And she's proud to showcase her culture on the world stage.

'Sikhi is super important to me, and it always will be,' she says. 'I like to encourage that you don't have to lose your identity. Be proud of where you come from. It's only going to propel you forward. I say certain prayers before I go out there. I speak to God, kind of saying, "We've done the work. Whatever your will is on the day, I accept it, but just let me do justice to my hard work and let me make my family proud." I think when you have that kind of empowerment, you feel fearless.'

As a world-class athlete, Karenjeet, who's also a chartered accountant, has undoubtedly established herself as a trailblazer and role model to her community and beyond.

'If I can encourage girls, especially from diverse minority backgrounds, to get into strength sports, competing alongside me against the world's best, I think I've done a good job,' she says. 'Gone are the days when we need to say that girls are denied these kinds of opportunities. You're always going to get people making assumptions and judgments, but I just let my actions do the talking.'

LESSONS FOR GOOD MENTAL HEALTH: Be proud of your identity and heritage. Your faith can make you feel empowered and help you to reach great heights.

Questions to think about:

1. Karenjeet has strong parental support. How has this helped her? Who is your biggest supporter and how does this person motivate you?

2. Karenjeet's father is her coach. How does she describe their relationship? What are the similarities and differences between a coach and a father?

3. What challenges relating to discrimination did Karenjeet face and how did she overcome them?

4. What does Karenjeet mean by "never judge a book by its cover?"

KRIS KUMARI

KRIS KUMARI

'Small wins help you evolve'

Nutrition is the foundation of good health. Food is one of the keys to optimizing performance.

As a registered performance nutritionist and football coach, Kris Kumari has combined her love of sport with a passion for creating tailor-made nutritional strategies for individuals, teams and organizations.

'I played at grassroots level and wanted to be a professional footballer,' says Kris. 'My son was born with a food allergy; this triggered my interest in nutrition.'

Kris is Gujarati and studied Nutrition Sciences, however, that was not her original career path.

She had a career change from working as an actress and retrained in Performance Nutrition. In addition to gaining football coaching badges, she decided to upskill herself and studied for an MSc in Sports Science and Exercise Medicine and is also a UEFA B fitness coach.

Kris's journey put her in touch with athletes at all levels, from young athletes to weekend warriors, to sportsmen and -women competing at the regional and national level. She has also gained experience in supporting a team of players in the Scottish Women's Premier League.

'It gave me experience to build relationships and apply my knowledge in a practical setting,' says Kris. 'I did not take a direct traditional route. I diversified, explored, and experienced many routes.'

Kris's business, KK-Nutrition, and her physical performance and nutrition coaching offer a comprehensive service that includes designing practical educational resources, one-to-one consultations and interactive workshops. Her goal is to assess nutritional and physical performance needs and find practical and personalized ways to support her clients to enhance their sporting performance. She applies the same meticulous approach on the football field.

As a football coach, she plans and delivers sessions and provides nutrition workshops to players. Kris enjoys building relationships and working with the athlete, creating resources, researching and devising strategies to support the individual to achieve their performance goals and to have a positive impact.

Of course, as a mum, Kris's career is a balancing act – she has to meet family demands. But perhaps a bigger challenge is getting people to accept nutrition's crucial role in sports performance.

'It's challenging to influence people in some sports that may not be considered as a sport, such as parkour, on the role of nutrition,' she says. 'Sometimes it's a challenge to accept that nutrition may not be the priority at that time for some sports clubs, so getting full-time work can be challenging.'

Despite the hurdles, Kris is committed to unlocking her clients' and players' true potential. As her career has progressed, she's also learned some valuable lessons.

'Small wins help you evolve,' she says. This includes learning from failures and applying those learnings to keep moving forward.

LESSONS FOR GOOD MENTAL HEALTH: Be curious and find purpose to help navigate your journey and be ready to be adaptable. Adopt a good work ethic to help steer your way and develop resilience. Having relevant qualifications is one side of the coin, and the ability to develop human interaction skills is the other; this makes a good mix and helps to add value.

PERSONAL MESSAGE: 'Your path may be unconventional, your challenges significant, but the key is to unlock your true potential by embracing change and understanding your personal success. Much like a well-balanced diet, success is a blend of diverse ingredients. Be adaptable, learn from setbacks and celebrate small wins. Fuel your purpose with curiosity, strong work ethic and resilience. In your journey don't forget to nourish not only your body but also your mind; mental resilience is your invisible strength, and discover the power to transform obstacles into small victories.'

Questions to think about:

1. What does a healthy and balanced diet look like to you?

2. How is leading a healthy lifestyle important to your physical and mental health?

3. Can you name three habits that you embed within your life to maintain a good work ethic?

4. Kris talks about the importance of human interaction skills; why are these important and how do you use them?

MARIA JAMILA KHAN

MARIA JAMILA KHAN

'Mental health is so critical. Body and mind need to be on the same page to be able to perform your best'

Genetics can play a significant role in anyone's success, and Maria Jamila Khan's sporting pedigree is absolutely top class. Her grandfather, Hashim Khan, won the British Open Squash Championship four times during an illustrious career. Making a name for Pakistanan in squash, Hashim also served as the pillar of the 'Khan Squash Dynasty'. Meanwhile, her relative Jahangir Khan is widely regarded as the best squash player of all time!

Indeed, the Khan family, which originated in Pakistan, was a squash dynasty that dominated the sport from the 1950s through to the 1980s. However, Maria did not follow in the family's footsteps.

Born in the United States – where football, or soccer as it's known in America – is the most prominent women's sport, Maria gravitated towards the beautiful game. She initially started out as a goalkeeper, eventually playing Division I for the University of Denver collegiate team, the Denver Pioneers. And she was somewhat of a pioneer herself.

'Being raised in the US, I was the only one that looked like me on all my football teams,' says Maria. 'This experience motivated me to make football more available at a high level for South Asian women and girls.'

After completing her Bachelor's degree, Maria moved to the United Arab Emirates to pursue her Master's. And it was there, while playing for a local amateur side, that she transitioned into a midfielder.

In the Middle East, she learned more about the women's game in Pakistan and wanted to help its development in any way she could. Her enthusiasm and ability led to an invitation to the Pakistan Women's National Team training camp, which in turn earned her a spot on the team, and eventually a role as its captain.

'What I enjoy most about captaining the Pakistan Women's National Team is the ability to witness the resilience of my teammates as well as being part of their football journeys as we grow and develop women's football in Pakistan,' says Maria.

In addition to climbing the ladder of success in football, Maria is also a powerhouse in the business world. In addition to playing football full-time, Maria has risen through the corporate ranks in global multinational organizations such as Ford Motor Company.

'Working for a large corporate organization has also helped me in leading the country in women's football. I have learned leadership skills as well as empathy and the ability to empower those around me,' she says. 'I know that I still have a lot to learn but trying to prioritize self-care has the potential to benefit not only you, but your teammates as well. Making sure you are the best version of yourself will allow you to be there for others.'

Of course, as a footballer, you always have something to prove, and there have been hurdles for Maria to overcome. One of which is being accepted by Pakistan as *Pakistani*.

'Having been raised outside of the country, there has been some pushback as to my leadership style and ability to lead the team,' she says.

Despite the naysayers, Maria continues to prevail, even earning praise from the prime minister of Pakistan for one of her goals against Saudi Arabia.

So far, it's been quite a ride, giving Maria a world of experience to share with others who might want to forge an equally challenging path.

LESSONS FOR GOOD MENTAL HEALTH: Surround yourself with a support system that genuinely believes in you and wants the best for you. As you grow, life will only become more difficult. It will not get easier but try to get better at your ability to handle hard obstacles.

PERSONAL MESSAGE: 'Find something you are passionate about and work relentlessly towards leaving that space better than you found it.'

Questions to think about:

1. Even though Maria didn't see any women that looked like her on her team, she still persevered. What attributes would Maria embody to allow her to remain determined? How can you use some of these attributes?

2. Maria speaks about developing leadership skills which she has used in her role as captain. Can you list your top five leadership skills? Write a reason beside each.

3. Maria moved from one country to another and is now a powerhouse in football and business. If you were to migrate to another country, where would you go and why?

4. What does 'relentless' mean and what can you do to leave a better space for others?

MOHINI BHARDWAJ

MOHINI BHARDWAJ

'I think the moment that I walked into the gym, I just realized that it was my passion, and that I loved it.'

Born in Philadelphia, USA, to an Indian father and a Russian mother, Mohini Bhardwaj was raised in Cincinnati where she discovered gymnastics at age five.

'I basically got started because there was somebody at my kindergarten that was tumbling, and I thought it was really cool, and I wanted to try it,' says Mohini. 'And at first, my mum said no. I think maybe a week or so later, she caught me trying to jump backwards onto a bunch of pillows off the bed and ended up putting me in class immediately after that.'

Mohini, whose name in Sanskrit means 'someone who mesmerizes', proved to be a gymnast well worth watching.

'You have certain kids that movement is involved with everything they do, and they actually learn more and their brain functions better with bouncing around and moving,' says Mohini. 'Doing gymnastics was a good way for me to funnel all of that energy and that movement into something that was a lot of fun.'

At thirteen, Mohini felt she needed more advanced training, so she asked her parents if she could move to Orlando, Florida, to train with a renowned coach. Breaking with tradition, her parents agreed.

Mohini lived with the family of another gymnast but soon became lonely. So, while her dad continued working in Cincinnati, her mum and younger brother went to live with her in a Florida apartment.

'My parents were like the Rock of Gibraltar. They stood solidly behind me and backed me to the hilt,' says Mohini.

By the age of sixteeen, Mohini was training with top gymnastics coach Alexander Alexandrov. And when he moved to Houston, Texas, she persuaded her parents to let her follow him.

Living alone in Houston proved to be challenging, but also an opportunity for growth as a young adult.

'Maybe I wasn't ready to handle things as well as I thought I could. I was a teenager with my own apartment', Mohini says.

Mohini would fail to make the 1995 US world championship and the 1996 U.S. Olympic teams. She wasn't realizing her potential, though she did get a college scholarship at UCLA. And after a shaky first year, she finally began to thrive.

She'd win two NCAA team titles and several individual medals. She also won a bronze as US team captain at the 2001 world championships. And in 2004, she crowned her twelve-year gymnastics journey with a landmark team silver medal at the Olympics.

'I actually had no idea that I was the first Indian-American gymnast to get a medal,' says Mohini. 'It was kind of a surprise to me. It's not something I sat out to necessarily accomplish. I think it just came with my hard work, and it just happened to fall that way.'

Mohini retired from competitive gymnastics in 2005 and was later inducted into the USA Gymnastics Hall of Fame. She's now a gym owner and coach in Oregon, and her advice to others is simple.

'My aha moment would be the fact that I was never really afraid of learning anything as far as gymnastics. A lot of people have fear and mental blocks that prevent them from learning really hard skills, and for me, I would just do things to see what would happen.'

LESSONS FOR GOOD MENTAL HEALTH: Don't fear trying something different as you never know where it might lead you.

Questions to think about:

1. How did Mohini initially get into gymnastics?

2. Mohini says that brain function can improve through moving around. What do you do to help your brain function, and can you describe the benefit of this strategy?

3. Why do you think living alone at sixteen proved to be challenging? Can you think of a time when you have felt lonely and what you did to provide comfort in this situation?

4. If you could try something of your choice, what would it be and why?

NAZIRA YUSUF

NAZIRA YUSUF

'Surround yourself with good people who will support you.'

'Choose a job you love, and you will never have to work a day in your life,' so the saying goes. And if your job combines two of your greatest loves, well, you're on easy street. Growing up in the UK in a British Asian family, Nazira Yusuf had a pair of passions – football and social media.

'I support Liverpool FC and have been going to watch them on a weekly basis since I was thirteen years old,' says Nazira. 'When I left college at age seventeen, I made the decision to seek a career in sports journalism.'

Though inspired by a female TV presenter on BT Sport, Nazira's ambitions lay in the digital media market. So, aged nineteen, she enrolled in the University Campus of Football & Business, the world's first higher-education institution to offer degrees in the football and sports industries.

'I studied MultiMedia Sports Journalism and received a first-class BA Honours,' she says. 'During my degree, I participated in a lot of voluntary work, managing social media platforms for my local grassroots football club for four years while also managing social media platforms for UCFB football teams. As social media manager for my grassroots football club, my job is to update the social media platforms on a daily basis and plan content for social media which will allow us to increase interaction and gain more followers and keep everyone updated on the football teams.'

As an ambitious graduate, Nazira picks up real-world experience wherever she can, from freelancing at BBC Sport to interning as a social media officer with Bolton United FC. However, while her career is burgeoning, it hasn't been without challenges.

'For me personally, it hasn't been an easy journey being female and from an under-represented background. I have had to work a lot harder as we are overlooked for so many positions especially having the stereotype of females not understanding sport at the level males do.'

To network and increase her understanding of the industry, Nazira joined BCOMS, the Black Collective of Media in Sport, a Black-led organization that works to create more diversity in the UK sports media.

'I met many inspiring people who currently work within the sports media industry and gained valuable advice and insight into their journeys and what it's like to work within football,' she says.

Like the athletes in the sports she covers, Nazira has to be mentally tough. Sports media is a demanding business requiring determination and sometimes a thick skin. But Nazira believes if you pick the right partners on your journey, things will all work out. This has led her to become a video journalist for HaytersTV where she attends pre- and post-match press conferences for teams in the Premier League.

'Surround yourself with good people who will support you because it's not an easy journey, but once you reach your highest point, you will be grateful you did.'

Of course, Nazira's journey is just getting started, but her progress is already inspirational to other ethnic-minority females who have an eye on a sports media career.

LESSONS FOR GOOD MENTAL HEALTH: Never give up on your dreams; instead, use your differences to others as motivation to break down barriers and become an inspiration for someone else. You never know who is watching your journey.

PERSONAL MESSAGE: 'If you really mean it, then don't give up. It's a long-haul career. Experience is what you need. Start in a smaller market. . . Small-market newspaper or radio, or a grassroots football club, non-league. Keep in mind that a LOT of people, even a lot of experienced journalists, want to do sports. If you are BETTER than everybody else around you, always available, always say yes. . . you might slowly move up. Network with others. It can be a cool job, but it requires a lot of sacrifice and understanding of what the job requires.'

Nazira Yusuf

Questions to think about:

1. Nazira speaks of her love for football and social media. What do you love doing and why?

2. Nazira's role involves using social media. It is important that you use social media platforms in a safe manner and report anything that makes you feel uncomfortable. Can you write down five top tips for keeping safe online?

3. What does the term stereotype mean and how has this affected Nazira?

4. Nazira spent much time volunteering. Why is volunteering important and how has this helped her in her journey?

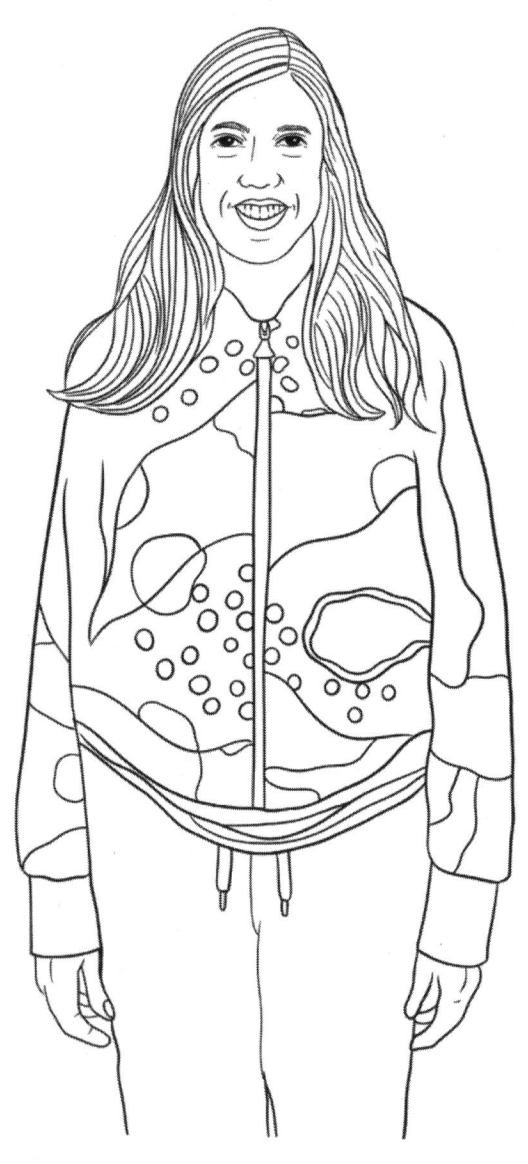

NOORAFSHAN MIRZA

NOORAFSHAN MIRZA

'Follow your passions in life. Trust in your instincts. Above all, believe in yourself!'

The pandemic was a moment of stagnation for many. But for Noorafshan Mirza, a British Muslim born of Indian and Pakistani heritage, lockdown presented a golden opportunity for some career development.

'I became a student of football during the lockdowns of 2020, watching games, webinars, listening to players, podcasts, and learning about the pathways into a career in sport,' says Noorafshan.

Noorafshan's passion for football seems like a radical departure from her initial career, which found her working in the arts. However, it was while engaged in an arts and culture project overseas that her interest in football was born.

'I was introduced to football through my friendships with Ghanaian athletes I met through my community when I was living in Istanbul,' she says. 'I instantly connected with their desires, talent, and hard work to pursue one's dreams. As an elite player myself (from a different industry), I had the realization that artists and athletes are kindred spirits expressing ourselves through our bodies, creating culture on/off the pitch.'

Having been bitten by the football bug, Noorafshan began playing and carving a niche off the field using her skills from the arts world, in which she was an expert in mentoring and coaching young talent, relationship building, and partnership work.

'I am now a licensed FA intermediary being encouraged into mentoring and representation, studying for my FIFA agents exam this year,' she says. 'I play in a grassroots women and non-binary team called Hot Flush FC in the Super 5 League. I volunteer for Clapton Community FC, and I am also currently stepping into coaching with Frenford & MSA women F.C.'

As a player's agent and director of NSOMASPORTS, a management agency that supports and promotes underserved talent in the arts and sports industries, Noorafshan's work is full of variety.

'My job entails a lot of different roles from communication, mindset and energy coaching, filming and producing player profiles, contract negotiations, to player care off the pitch, family support, networking, creating new opportunities, partnership collaboration, travelling, scouting, and talent ID,' she says.

Noorafshan was already a high-achiever when she got into the football business, but that doesn't mean her role is without challenges.

'As an agent working on your own in a team sport, I have found it is quite a lonely and misunderstood place to exist in the ecology of the game. The overall sentiment towards agents is quite negative. General awareness is focused towards a minority of (mostly male) super agents that make a lot of money. Therefore, the general opinion is that agents take a lot out and don't give back to the game. [But] positively, I do feel there is a big cultural shift happening within the business of representation, and I'm excited about being part of the change.' Becoming part of the solution obviously requires some mental toughness, but Noorafshan believes it's a marriage of mind and body that will help you achieve your goals.

'Mindset-and-energy work (gratitude, yoga, affirmations, meditation) has helped me shape the way I see myself and, in turn, transform the negative experiences I had growing up that contributed to my sense of low self-worth,' she says. 'Being in my body connects me to the present, to the moment of non-thinking and just being, a feeling of lightness. That's why I love playing football.'

Being a woman, an ethnic minority and an agent in the football world, Noorafshan has some well-established preconceptions to overcome. But she's making it happen. And her message to anyone with a dream is simply to go for it!

LESSONS FOR GOOD MENTAL HEALTH: Follow your passions in life. What you love most, pour your heart and soul into. This provides a route in. Trust in your instincts and be guided by your intuition. Above all, believe in yourself!

PERSONAL MESSAGE: 'Learn about what you love, find and create community, and keep believing!'

Noorafshan Mirza

Questions to think about:

1. Noorafshan describes similarities between artists and athletes. What are these similarities and do any of these characteristics resonate with you?

2. What have you learned are some of the key roles of a football agent?

3. What do you understand by mental toughness and how do you think Noorafshan demonstrates this in her role?

4. Playing football is a way of helping Noorafshan maintain positive energy. What do you do to help you remain positive and why?

PREETI SHETTY

RUQSANA BEGUM

PREETI SHETTY

'Doing something you believe in makes the hard days a little bit easier.'

Preeti Shetty's trail-blazing role in football began when she capitalized on a happy accident. Born to a South Asian family in Dubai, she completed a Media and Communications degree in London which led to a life-changing opportunity at the BBC.

'I got a work experience position at BBC Sport working on an outreach project called BBC Your Game,' says Preeti. 'This gave me my first insight and experience into the power sport has to change lives and communities. I knew then I never wanted to do anything else ever again, and I actively looked for sport development organisations where I could learn more and add value.'

After gaining some real-world experience, Preeti did a Master's degree in Sports Management and the Business of Football and later a postgraduate diploma focused on Sport and Social Change. A role at the large sports charity The Football Foundation soon followed. There she became head of an online impact measurement system called Upshot.

Having been the head of Upshot at the Football Foundation for several years, the pandemic gave her the opportunity to buy Upshot from the Foundation and set it up as an independent social enterprise.

Preeti says, 'At Upshot, we work with over 1400 sports organizations and non-profits, helping them manage their programmes, monitor their progress, and evidence their impact. We do this by giving them access to a software we built which allows them to collect good data and report back to their stakeholders and funders. We also support them in building their own skills, knowledge, and capacity through consultancy services.'

Alongside her work at Upshot, Preeti built her knowledge and credibility by joining several boards. She became the vice chair of Street Child United, advocating for the rights of street-connected children using the power of sport. She was appointed director for London Sport, a charity that encourages Londoners to be more active. And most groundbreaking of all, she became the first British South Asian woman to claim a seat in a Premier League boardroom when she was named as a director of Brentford Football Club.

'My favourite part of my role is the range of organizations I get to work with and the satisfaction I get from seeing the difference they are making in their communities,' Preeti explains. 'With my non-executive board positions, I really enjoy contributing towards developing organizational strategies, supporting on equality, diversity and inclusion plans, and building purposeful teams that care about having meaningful impact.'

Board positions are an incredible opportunity for her to contribute her skills to organizations and causes that she cares about and help her develop and grow as an individual and a leader.

Preeti's rise to the top might seem smooth, but challenges always exist.

'Being a female CEO in the sports and tech world can be very isolating, and I find juggling my many responsibilities and ensuring I am adding value to all is always a struggle,' she says.

Hard work, mental toughness, and the ability to make the most of her opportunities have kept Preeti's career on an upward trajectory, making her an ideal role model for those hoping to follow in her footsteps.

'Learn all aspects of the industry and then find a niche,' she says. 'Find your purpose, your why. Doing something you really believe in makes the hard days a little bit easier.'

LESSONS FOR GOOD MENTAL HEALTH: Don't put too much pressure on yourself. There is no defined time to be successful. And build a great network of people around you who you can trust and who will tell you the hard truths.

PERSONAL MESSAGE: 'Embark on a career path where your passion and purpose align. Seek out roles that challenge you, push you to grow, and allow you to contribute to something larger than yourself. Embrace learning and collaboration, as these are the cornerstones of innovation and change. Be open to diverse perspectives and experiences, as they will enrich your understanding and approach. Your journey may not always be easy, but it will be meaningful. You have the power to create change, inspire others, and leave a lasting legacy.'

Questions to think about:

1. Preeti speaks about how sport has the power to change lives. What power do you think sport has and why?

2. What key attributes would be needed to be in the position of 'director' and how would these attributes be used?

3. Preeti talks about building purposeful teams. If you could choose four people to be in your work team, who would they be and why?

4. Have you thought about what drives you to wake up each morning and do what you do? What motivates you and how does that link to your moral purpose?

RUQSANA BEGUM

'Talent is nothing without sacrifice'

Ruqsana Begum has been fighting for much of her life. A London-born Bangladeshi, she was raised in a strict Muslim family where her love of sport was at odds with her parents' expectations.

'I knew I was good at sports from a very young age,' Ruqsana says. 'But it was also unheard of for someone from my background to participate in sports. There were hardly any Muslim women playing sports. I used to love playing football. [But] as soon as I became ten or eleven, my mum didn't let me go out to play with the boys. She wanted me to study and help her in the kitchen.'

But Ruqsana's love of sport refused to die. And at eighteen, she secretly took up Muay Thai kickboxing.

'I was in university, but I was afraid to tell them because I thought if I informed them, they wouldn't let me go to the gym,' she says. Soon, Ruqsana's hobby became a passion.

'I do love it,' she says. 'Stepping into the ring allows you to grow because you're putting yourself in such depths of fear. And when you overcome that, there's such a sense of accomplishment. I love that and the fact I'm constantly working towards my goal and progressing, even if I sometimes lose.'

For almost five years, Ruqsana hid the truth from her family. Mentally, the deceit was a challenge, as was the bullying she endured from other girls at the gym. But she persevered, with her growing skills giving her a sense of self.

'I think any creative art form, whether music or dance, Muay Thai or boxing, allows you to channel emotion and express yourself,' she says. 'I was fortunate to have discovered Thai boxing when I had few other opportunities to express myself. I found my passion in life and realized I was good at it. But it's like anything in life – talent is nothing without sacrifice.'

However, despite her sacrifice, a reckoning was just around the corner.

At twenty-three, Ruqsana's parents set up a traditional arranged marriage.

'It was overwhelming,' Ruqsana recalls. 'I thought: "Whoa, I need to take a breath because I don't even know him." I felt so much pressure to go along with it. So, I tried to speak to my mum. She waved me away and was very dismissive. They made it clear this was going to happen.' The unwanted marriage forced Ruqsana to quit kickboxing, which took a heavy toll on her psyche.

'I was on antidepressants for four months and completely bedridden. But I didn't want to be on antidepressants because they numb you. The only thing I remembered enjoying was Muay Thai, and so I told myself: "Get back to the gym,"' she says.

It was then that she finally confessed all to her parents.

'At that point, they realized that it was healthy for me to do gym,' she says. 'My dad was very understanding when my doctor explained to him. Then he let me get back to the gym. My parents were very kind during that time.'

Her husband eventually filed for divorce and thereafter, Ruqsana's kickboxing career flourished. She went on to win a bronze medal for the UK at the world championship, gold at the 2012 European Championship, and was crowned world champion in 2016. It was a fitting reward for all she'd endured.

'When I had all those problems, I didn't blame others,' she says. 'I took responsibility and said: "OK, this is where I am. How do I move forward?" I found the best way to heal myself is through sport. So, I'm really grateful for having Muay Thai and now boxing in my life.'

LESSONS FOR GOOD MENTAL HEALTH: Try not to blame others and find something to focus on that can help you overcome your problems.

PERSONAL MESSAGE: 'The journey of life is getting to know yourself and evolve through challenges and obstacles. It's there to test you and elevate you, so embrace it and move through it with conviction and confidence.'

Questions to think about:

1. Ruqsana speaks of not seeing many Muslim women playing sport when she was growing up. How did this make her feel and how did she use this to become a role model for others?

2. There are many trail-blazing Muslim women in Sport. Can you find out the names of five Muslim women who are championing sport and write a little bit about the sport they represent?

3. Quitting kickboxing took a toll on Ruqsana's emotional health. What strategies can you use to help you maintain a positive mindset during tough times?

4. Ruqsana was crowned world champion in 2016. Having been through challenging times, she was determined to succeed. What does this tell you about her character? How could you use some of those traits in your life?

SANNAH ADAM

SANNAH ADAM

'Do what you enjoy, not what others expect of you.'

Sannah Adam is a force of nature, in the boxing ring and out of it. 'At the age of fourteen, I started the Duke of Edinburgh Award (silver), and it required an hour of physical activity each week for six months to complete the award,' says Sannah. 'At the time, my brother decided to start boxing as a hobby, and my parents encouraged me to do the same.'

Alongside boxing, Sannah was also a star in the classroom and a born leader. 'Ever since leaving St Paul's Primary with the Deane Ambassador of the Year award and being deputy head girl of Sharples School, I've always found myself in a leading position and listening to other people's ideas and needs to make something better.' Sannah's gift for leadership was soon apparent at the gym.

'By the age of around eighteen/nineteen, I was already doing what a boxing coach does. I would hold the pads. I knew the techniques of how to throw punches. And being around boxers, I pretty much knew their daily routine too.'

At twenty, Sannah became a certified England boxing coach and began offering female-only boxing sessions at her local club.

'I started off initially with my first class of around fifteeen girls and consistently had a class each week,' she says. 'I had received lots of messages of positivity and uplifting comments. Things like "It's so nice to see such a young Asian girl doing so much for the girls in our community." I knew at this point I had definitely changed attitudes towards females in boxing and sport in general because of all the feedback I was getting.' Over time Sannah's classes have grown and she is now coaching around forty to fifty girls a week.

Despite her success at the gym, Sannah still maintained her studies. In 2022, she graduated from the University of Law in Manchester. And she hasn't stopped there.

As a law graduate, Sannah's dual career involves coaching, while being a project coordinator for Inspire Capital Sports. She is also involved in public speaking at schools, colleges, and universities, speaking about how she manages being a boxing coach alongside working and studying.

In November 2023, Sannah became the winner of the 'Rising Star' for the She Inspires Awards, following being a two-category finalist and winner of Young Achiever of the Year 2022. Sannah's progress may appear seamless, but it's not been without challenges.

'Being a female from a South Asian background, sport was never particularly encouraged or considered as a "proper" career path for women,' says Sannah. 'When I started boxing initially, I faced many comments from other people such as "You're a girl, why do you do boxing?" The best thing I did was blur out these attitudes and comments.

In the prime of her twenties, Sannah is already an experienced trail-blazer with a wealth of advice for others.

For anyone who is aspiring to work in sport or be a sports person, she says that 'you should always be ready to absorb your surroundings like a sponge. Having a genuine passion about the sport or field you'd like to pursue as well as always being prepared to meet others who have years of experience is important.'

Sannah feels that you have to be far more disciplined than the average person and have a strong mind. Whether you're male or female, everyone at some point gets some form of negativity.

However, you have to be thick-skinned and remind yourself why you chose to pursue it in the first place.

LESSONS FOR GOOD MENTAL HEALTH: You have to be confident in yourself and really be careful of where you put your energy or what you spend time doing. Do what you enjoy, not what others expect of you.

PERSONAL MESSAGE: 'Turn your passions into a fire nobody can extinguish.'

S. Adam

Questions to think about:

1. What are the character traits of a good leader?

2. As a woman, what challenges did Sannah face when she started boxing and how did she overcome them?

3. Sannah has been able to maintain a dual career. What is a dual career and how do you think she has been able to manage boxing and law?

4. What do you do to keep a strong mind?

SHAMEEMA M. YOUSUF

SHAMEEMA M. YOUSUF

'Develop qualities and strengths to support resiliency and self-care.'

Shameema M. Yousuf is a dynamic powerhouse. A dual British and Zimbabwean citizen of Indian heritage, she's enjoyed a trio of demanding careers. And with each switch of focus, she's had success!

'I was an elite international-level athlete,' she says. 'I retrained to become a psychologist in sport after sixteen years as a commodities trader/fund manager in high-performance investment banking environments.'

Though she didn't have a role model, Shameema was blessed with passion, determination, and a strong desire to help people. She also had a massive thirst for knowledge.

'I have a Bachelor of Social Science joint honours majoring in Economics and Accountancy as well as a Master of Science in Business Finance confirmed in the UK,' she says. 'I then gained a Master of Education in Clinical Counselling specializing in Sport and Performance Psychology at Boston University, USA.

After twelve years of successful practice, I have now gone into academia and am doing my doctoral research at the University of South Carolina, USA, while still maintaining some practice.

'Although an unorthodox route, it enabled my current licensure and registrations through British associations. I now serve as an Association for Applied Sport Psychology (USA) Executive Board leader of which I am member.'

Shameema's breathtaking list of qualifications is the foundation for a sports psychology career that includes more than a decade of private practice and numerous prestigious roles within professional bodies. It's also taken her into the minds of a diverse array of clients. As a practitioner, she works one-on-one with athletes and coaches (primarily in football, tennis, and motorsport) to support performance and well-being, support team dynamics, and impact systems and culture at an organizational level in sport. She also supports C-suite leaders in the corporate industry in performance optimization and leadership culture.

Despite her impressive resumé, Shameema has faced the same prejudices and resistance many professional women encounter. And she believes being a woman of colour only made the hurdles higher.

'I was the only Muslim woman of colour HCPC-registered sport psychologist to my knowledge trying to progress. It impacted me financially and personally, but I persisted. This led to advocacy work in policy change in sport and psychology.'

In addition to ethnicity issues, Shameema also faced opposition to the very nature of what she did. As a sport psychologist, she felt that there was a stigma associated with her role. But with changing attitudes and recognition of the importance of mental skills and wellness for athletes and coaches, this has become less of a barrier.

During her three careers, Shameema has accumulated a wealth of knowledge. And she believes her experiences can be applied to life on and off the sports field. Shameema says that it is important to be passionate, intentional, and clear on your direction and ambitions. Building a diverse skillset and mastering your craft can help you forge multiple paths. Most importantly for Shameema, sport psychology is about helping people. She also feels that you should be unafraid to commit to equity and belonging through advocacy and she makes it a lifestyle choice in her research and practice.

Fittingly, when it comes to mental health, Shameema is a firm believer in combining teamwork with a strong sense of self. No one is an island, but self-sufficiency is a strength! Develop qualities and strengths to support resiliency and self-care and ensure that you are defined not only by what you do but by who you are.

LESSONS FOR GOOD MENTAL HEALTH: Surround yourself with good mentors and allies who support you during challenging times and promote you for opportunities.

PERSONAL MESSAGE: 'Social justice is a choice for those committed to inclusion, equity and belonging in a patriarchal global society. Be unafraid to lean into this choice via many conduits with the support of allies, and the development of your strengths.'

Shameema M. Yousuf

Questions to think about:

1. What is sport psychology and how does a sport psychologist help people?

2. Mental skills are tools for the mind. What mental skills do you use and how do they help you?

3. Who are C-suite leaders and what do they do?

4. What does the term equity mean and how would you benefit from equitable approaches?

SHANELL SALGADO

SHANELL SALGADO

'Success is the amount of times you get up and push through all challenges.'

Goalkeeper Shanell Salgado could hardly have chosen two bigger names to inspire her football dreams, as her childhood idols were serial winners and among the best in the history of the game.

'My inspiration to play football was mainly Ronaldinho. His finesse and trickery with the ball was always just jaw-dropping,' she says. 'And specifically to be a goalkeeper was Oliver Kahn. During major competitions, he would make incredible saves, and I remember wanting to dive like him.'

Shanell, whose parents are from Sri Lanka and Portugal, was born and raised in Germany, but saw her professional career blossom in England. 'I started off at Sunday leagues clubs and attended lots of trials with higher-level clubs,' she says. 'Eventually, I got into the championship in 2018. I played for Crystal Palace, Charlton, and Lewes and Blackburn Rovers.'

Becoming a professional footballer is the dream of many, but relatively few make it. South Asian players are thinner on the ground in the English pro ranks than most, which makes Shanell's success even more remarkable. But whatever your ethnic background, you only get there with the right mindset.

'A key aspect is your work ethic,' says Shanell. 'You must put the effort in on and off the pitch. It's a lifestyle that you need to follow and enjoy. Focus on what you want to achieve and where you want to go and go pursue it.'

As the last line of defence, Shanell's role carries huge responsibility. When she started out, goalkeepers were mainly regarded as shot-stoppers. However, in the modern game, the keeper has to be more of an all-round footballer, which means Shanell has had to adapt. 'The game has evolved, and I now use my feet much more when retaining possession of the ball, and it's helped me grow as a keeper,' she says. 'There are a lot of different coaching styles, and overall I always try to soak up as much as possible and apply what I learn in training and in games.'

Of course, football is a team game that extends far beyond the eleven players you see on the field. And as the saying goes, "There's no "I" in team," so Shanell believes people skills are very important.

'In the game, you will meet all sorts of characters. People that will support you, people that will challenge you, and people that will make you feel hurt,' she says. 'Always remind yourself of what is in your control and remember people come into your life for a season, a reason, or a lesson.'

Like all sports, football demands as much of you mentally as physically, and at the top level, there's no escaping pressure. Injury, coaching styles, switching clubs, or your relationship with your teammates can all influence your performance. However, Shanell believes it's how you deal with the ups and downs that's most significant.

LESSONS FOR GOOD MENTAL HEALTH: Success isn't the top; success is the amount of times you get up and push through all challenges.

PERSONAL MESSAGE: 'Accept failure, because there is always plenty of that on the road, but don't live with regret. There are always highs after going through low moments, and just keep the hope and be consistent. Keep high standards for yourself and have positive affirmations.'

Questions to think about:

1. Shanell speaks about focusing on what you want to achieve. Can you write down some of your goals and what you are going to do to help you achieve them?

2. Why is it important to be adaptable and how can adaptability help you in your life?

3. What do you understand by people skills? Make a list of five people skills that you think are important and provide a reason for each.

4. Failure is a big part of learning. What do you do to maintain a growth mindset and how does a growth mindset help you recover from setbacks?

GOAL SETTING

Goal setting will help you to think critically about your intentions in life. Goals help you to visualize what you want to achieve and teach you to take responsibility for your own learning and behaviours. With consistency, goal setting can become a powerful lifelong habit that helps you to live your life with focus, purpose and an 'I can do' attitude.

You may have a mixture of big and small goals. Big goals are long-term aspirations that may take you time to achieve.

Small goals can be stepping stones to achieve your big goal, although this might not always be the case but can be achieved in a shorter amount of time.

Remember, small steps can lead to big wins. It is important to remain persistent and, whenever things get a little tough, keep moving forward. The only way to turn your goals into a reality is to keep trying.

Write down your big and small goals below and opposite and think about the plan that you will put in place to help you achieve them.

GRATITUDE

Expressing gratitude on a regular basis can have a big effect on our lives. Did you know that brain research shows that positive emotions are good for our bodies, minds and brains? Positive emotions make us feel good about ourselves and boost our ability to learn and make good decisions.

Learning to be grateful also helps you to deal with adversity and build strong relationships by maintaining focus on good experiences.

Try to focus your attention on one good thing each day. Use the gratitude journal opposite to note what you are thankful for and why.

MINDFULNESS

Mindfulness helps you to build self-esteem, manage stress, and develop different ways of approaching challenges. Having a healthy mind will help you to keep focus, pay attention and notice what is happening around you and how it is making you feel.

Sometimes big feelings can be tricky to manage on your own. Building mindfulness practice into your daily habits can help you to become more aware of your thoughts and feelings. For example, deep breathing, exercise, reading and counting are just a few examples of what can help you to become more mindful. So, instead of being overwhelmed by big feelings, you are better able to manage them.

Use the weekly chart opposite to create your own mindfulness calendar.

RESILIENCE

Resilience is the ability to bounce back after challenges and difficulties. By demonstrating resilience you can recover from setbacks using a growth mindset and you are more willing to take healthy risks without fear of failure. Resilience develops when you experience adversity and learn to deal with these challenging situations positively.

You can demonstrate resilience by being brave, curious, managing strong emotions and reframing setbacks as opportunities for growth.

Can you write your own acrostic poem about how you demonstrate resilience?

R _____
E _____
S _____
I _____
L _____
I _____
E _____
N _____
C _____
E _____

DIKSHA DAGAR – FACT FILE

Diksha Dagar is an Indian professional golfer who is also hearing-impaired. She became the leading amateur ladies, golfer in India from November 2015.

Diksha represented India at the 2017 Summer Deaflympics where golf was included for the very first time and competed in the women's individual golf event securing a silver medal.

Diksha also qualified to represent India at the 2018 Asian Games and, in 2019, she became only the second Indian female golfer, after Aditi Ashok, to win the Ladies European Tour and became the youngest Indian woman to do so at the age of 18.

In July 2021, Diksha received a surprise invitation from the International Golf Federation to compete in the women's individual event at the 2020 Summer Olympics.

Diksha eventually became the first golfer ever in history to have competed in both Olympics and Deaflympics.

MARY KOM – FACT FILE

Mary Kom, nicknamed Magnificent Mary, is an Indian amateur boxer who belongs to the Kom tribal community in the north-eastern state of Manipur.

She is the only woman to win the World Amateur Boxing Championship six times, the only female boxer to have won a medal in each one of the first seven world championships, and the only boxer to win eight world championship medals.

She became the first Indian female boxer to win a gold medal in the Asian Games in 2014 at Incheon, South Korea, and at the 2018 Commonwealth Games.

Mary fought to overcome poverty she faced as a child to pursue her dreams and is a true role model for aspiring female boxers all over the world.

RUBINA CHHETRY – FACT FILE

Rubina Chhetry hails from Kakkarvitta, a neighbourhood of Mechinagar municipality in the district of Jhapa, eastern Nepal.

She was raised by her mother and from early childhood was attracted to sports.

Rubina is a Nepali cricketer who plays for the women's national cricket team as a right-arm medium pace bowler.

She has been the captain of the team since 2012, when she replaced Neri Thapa.

In 2009, she became the first cricketer to take a hat trick for Nepal in an international match, and in 2019 she took Nepal's first hat trick in a Women's Twenty20 International.

Although in her early years, she had difficulty in managing her cricket activities alongside her education and other commitments, inspired by her family, Rubina is now widely considered to be one of the greatest female cricket players ever in Nepal.

SANIA MIRZA – FACT FILE

Sania Mirza was born in Mumbai, to Hyderabadi Muslim parents. She is a former professional tennis player who represented India.

Sania is also a former doubles world number 1 and won six major titles – three in women's doubles and three in mixed doubles.

From 2003 until her retirement from singles in 2013, she was ranked by the Women's Tennis Association as the Indian Number one in singles.

Starting her journey as a youngster at a time when there was a lack of pathways for her to become a tennis professional, through sacrifice, determination and resilience, she turned her talent into a successful career.

Sania, with family support, defied all odds to fulfil her dreams. She is an icon for many young girls and women who have the desire to become an international athlete.

©Kym Elder

MANISHA TAILOR is a renowned award-winning UEFA A-licensed football coach and author of *Dream Like Me: South Asian Football Trailblazers*. She has a background in primary education and trained as a head-teacher before embarking on a career in football. Through her community outreach work she uses education and football as a vehicle to positively influence change within the game. Manisha's work has had global impact having delivered keynote addresses at international conferences in several countries across Asia and Canada. Tailor holds advisory roles with the Football Association, the League Coaches Association and Sporting Equals. She received an MBE in 2017 for services to football and diversity in sport.

ACKNOWLEDGEMENTS

Allyship, for me and many of the pioneering women in this book, has been essential in the fight for gender equality and empowerment.

I want to thank all those who have been actively supporting, advocating for and collaborating with women and marginalized genders to help create a more inclusive society. Organizations that I have closely worked with include Indian Gymkhana, Muslimah Sports Association, the Football Association, Kick it Out and Sporting Equals who work tirelessly to ensure that sport is truly for all.

To all our amazing professionals included in this book, thank you for your pioneering work in the world of sport. I am grateful to those who were able to provide a personal message to the reader and sign off their stories included in this book. Unfortunately, despite my very best efforts, I was unable to track down some of our inspiring women for their personal stories and signatures.

For all the trail-blazing women who have and are continuing to inspire generations of women and girls to dream big, challenge the status quo, and make a difference in the world.

OTHER HOPEROAD YOUNG ADULT TITLES YOU MIGHT ENJOY

THE WILD ONES

Antonio Ramos Revillas
Translated by Claire Storey

Fifteen-year-old Efraín and his two younger brothers live in a house on the hillside in Monterrey, northern Mexico. They are left to fend for themselves after their mother is wrongly arrested for theft.
Má has raised her boys to keep out of trouble with the local gangs and to study for their future, but they are viewed by society as good-for-nothings or criminals simply because of where they live. The only people offering any kind of support are the local gang members – but everything comes with a price tag.

978-1-913109-34-9

THE DARKNESS OF COLOURS

Martín Blasco
Translated by Claire Storey

The Darkness of Colours is a historical thriller narrated from two different perspectives, in two eras. The main event, around which the novel revolves, is the kidnapping of five children during the night of 5 April 1885. This is the start of the experiment into the idea of nature vs nurture. What happens if these children are given different upbringing?

Twenty-five years after the kidnapping, the children, now grown up, suddenly reappear on the doorsteps of their biological parents. Confused by his daughter's memory loss, one parent hires a journalist to investigate. Will he discover what has happened to his daughter and the other children? And why have they suddenly reappeared after all this time?

978-1-913109-33-2

29 LOCKS

Nicola Garrard

Coming-of-age novel set in contemporary London and Hertfordshire. Fifteen-year-old Donald Leroy Samson is the son of an absentee St Lucian father and a drug-addicted English mother. Growing up in dire poverty in Hackney, East London, his life is shaped by casual violence, gang initiation, drug-dealing and knife crime. When Donny's bored, rich, white girlfriend Zoe is offered a dubious modelling audition, the couple 'borrow' a barge and navigate the twenty-nine locks on the canal system from Hertfordshire down into Kings Cross.
When they start out on their journey, the future for both of them looks unpromising, like the fake audition, but as each lock is navigated and conquered, as the waters fall then rise again, their adventure takes on a new dimension. Life will never be the same again. A gritty, urban tale of redemption

978-1-913109-84-4

21 MILES

Nicola Garrard

21 Miles revisits the much-loved protagonist of *29 Locks* two years after his canal boat adventure as a fifteen-year-old. Older, wiser and more confident, life is going well for the former gang member who's escaped a brutal life of criminal exploitation. But when Donny and his best friend Zoe plan a day trip to France ahead of their sixth-form exams, Donny loses his passport and is arrested as an 'illegal' migrant.

To survive, he must rely on the help of unaccompanied teenage refugees, living rough in the dunes east of Calais. Can Donny use his boat skills to cross the busiest shipping channel in the world and make it home?

978-1-913109-21-9

NEVER TELL ANYONE YOUR NAME

Federico Ivanier
Translated by Claire Storey

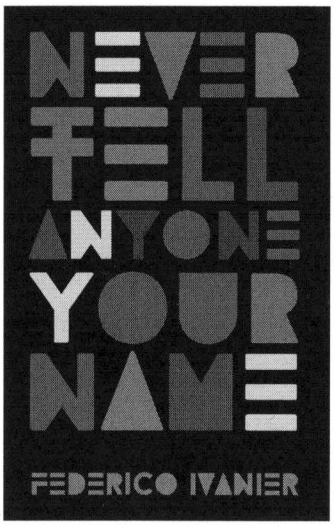

A Uruguayan teenager, travelling alone from France to Spain, finds he has accidentally booked the wrong train to Madrid. While he waits for the next train, he finds himself in the Spansh border town of Irún with eight hours to kill. Embracing the night, he roams the deserted streets listening to music and contemplating the sweetheart he left behind in Uruguay until he is befriended by a girl about his age. At first there is the thrill of new connection, but as the night wears on she seems less friendly than at first she appeared. The plot twists and turns and only the shocking conclusion reveals if train will leave with the boy aboard.

978-1-913109-22-6

THE SILENT STRIKER

Pete Kalu

Marcus is the best player in his football team. He's so good that there's a very real chance he'll be signed by Manchester United. But when he discovers he may be losing his hearing, his whole world falls to pieces and he finds himself having to put them back together on his own. But is this feeling of isolation real or just a consequence of his own behaviour? While dealing with parents, friends and first girlfriends, Marcus gradually understands that accepting the help of others is ultimately an acceptance of self.
A novel about friendship and family, *The Silent Striker* explores the issue of disability, and deafness, and the different ways in which we can choose to handle it.

978-1-908446-69-5